H is for Helping Others

Author: Dr. C. White-Elliott

Illustrated by: Ariana Halverson

www.clfpublishing.org
909.315.3161

Illustrations by Ariana Halverson. Contact info: AHalver3rs0n@gmail.com

Cover design by Senir Design. Contact info: info@senirdesign.com

ISBN # 978-1-945102-42-4

Printed in the United States of America.

"Two are better than one, because they have a good return for their labor: If either of them falls down, one can help the other up. But pity anyone who falls and has no one to help them up. Also, if two lie down together, they will keep warm. But how can one keep warm alone? Though one may be overpowered, two can defend themselves. A cord of three strands is not quickly broken" (Ecclesiastes 4:9-12, NIV).

God designed people and animals to work together to complete tasks in their home and/or their natural habitat. People complete tasks together in their communities, in their homes, and on their jobs. Let's look around our world and see how animals help each other.

Rayna, a mother bear, helps her cubs live longer by protecting them and keeping them safe. She provides safety by placing herself between her cubs and the danger.

Barney, the dog, helps his friend Wiggles, the dog, dig a hole to bury his bone. And, they have fun together while they do it.

Sammy, the kitten, decided to be adventurous and climb a tree. Then, he was too scared to come down. His mother Tabby heard him crying, so she climbed up the tree to save him.

Penelope, the mother elephant, gives her children a bath in the lake after they have finished playing in the mud.

Robin's baby birds were crying from hunger.
They are too young to fly yet and find their
own food. To soothe their tummies, she feeds
her hungry babies nice plumb worms.

The butterfly has an awesome job of helping nature. Look how she helps to pollinate the beautiful flower.

The bunny rabbits run around helping each other find food. They like to eat vegetables, such as cabbage, lettuce, and even carrots. They play a game of tag as they go.

Some birds must migrate during winter. When it's time to fly south, they have a leader that leads the school of birds from the cold climate to a warmer one.

Remember, when you see a person or an animal in need, do what you can to help. We are all on God's green other, and we must help one another.

www.ingramcontent.com/pod-product-compliance
Lightning Source LLC
Chambersburg PA
CBHW041957100426
42813CB00019B/2909